Other books by Kate Salley Palmer
published by Warbranch Press, Inc.

A Gracious Plenty (ISBN 9780966711400)
The Pink House (ISBN 9780966711417)
The Little Chairs (ISBN 9780966711424)
Palmetto – Symbol of Courage (ISBN 9780966711448)
Francis Marion and the Legend of the Swamp Fox (ISBN 9780966711455)
Almost Invisible – Black Patriots of the American Revolution
(ISBN 9780966711462)

www.warbranchpress.com

Text copyright © 2013 by Kate Salley Palmer and Jim Palmer
Art copyright © 2013 by James H. Palmer, Jr.

The illustrations were produced digitally on a MacBook Pro
Printed in the USA by Electric City Printing, Anderson, South Carolina

ISBN 9780966711479

Published by Warbranch Press, Inc.
329 Warbranch Road
Central, SC 29633

First Printing

For the descendants of
the first South Carolinians
                    --Kate and Jim Palmer

For Mike Biggs
                    --James H. Palmer, Jr.

FIRST SOUTH CAROLINIANS

Written by Kate Salley Palmer &
Jim Palmer

Illustrated by James H. Palmer Jr.

People have been living on the North American continent for about 40,000 years.

Scholars believe that the first people migrated across a thick layer of ice from Asia to present-day Alaska. After crossing this Ice Age "land bridge" many people continued heading south and southeast, hunting game such as the woolly mammoth along the way. These early people were nomadic; they didn't stay in one place very long, always moving in search of food.

Ice age hunters bringing down a great mammoth

Archaic Indian family

As the earth grew warmer and the ice began to melt, the great herds of mammoth began to disappear. People continued heading south, many settling in what is now the state of South Carolina. They began to hunt smaller game, such as deer, bear and other small animals. They also gathered nuts and other plants to eat. This led to basic farming and cultivating of crops.

Woodland Period pottery
with fish and oysters

During what is known as the **Woodland Period**, the early people of South Carolina established more permanent villages. It was during this time that people first began to make and fire pottery to use in cooking and in carrying water and other materials.

Fish and oysters were a major source of food for the early native people who settled along the coastal rivers and streams of South Carolina during the Woodland period.

Later, about 1,200 years ago, during what is known as the **Mississippian Period**, settlements in South Carolina grew more permanent and became villages. There were great advancements in agriculture during this time as well. People cultivated crops such as corn, squash, beans, peas, melons and other seed-bearing plants. One interesting feature of this period is the practice of mound building. The large mounds varied in shape and sometimes had houses or other structures on top. The people also conducted various ceremonies on top of the mounds.

The first Mississippian settlements in South Carolina appeared along the Savannah River. Eventually, people settled farther inland, mostly on bluffs or hills overlooking streams.

A Mississippian
mound and warrior

HOW DO WE KNOW ABOUT NATIVE SOUTH CAROLINIANS?

Most of what we know about how the early native people of South Carolina lived comes from Europeans who first made contact with them more than 500 years ago. This is the period of First Contact. While the European explorers did, in fact, treat the early Native Americans very badly, they provided a written account of the customs, living habits, and general appearance of the people they found.

Explorers described the native people as "well-proportioned (well-formed) and handsome" with reddish-brown skin color. The Europeans reported that the natives had great strength and endurance without appearing very muscular. Most of the men were tall, around six feet (the Cherokee were the tallest), with dark hair and piercing eyes. No facial hair or beards were observed, and some tribes wore only a tuft of hair on the crown of the head, with the other hair shaved off or torn out by the roots (a Cherokee practice).

Cherokee man and woman

Edisto man from the coastal region

Some tribes, especially along the coast, wore headbands with shells or feathers attached. They also practiced tattooing of their bodies.

The women and some men of the coastal tribes wore necklaces made of shells. Men wore a band tied around their hips, which supported a length of cloth or deerskin draped between their legs, the ends of the garment falling in flaps in front and back. Women often wore clothes made of deerskin. In the Coastal Plain region, some added Spanish moss as clothing. Most native people wore deerskin moccasins, but many went without shoes of any kind.

Body painting was a very important part of tribal life for many native people. It was often used on special occasions, such as before going into battle or before playing games.

Cherokee body painting

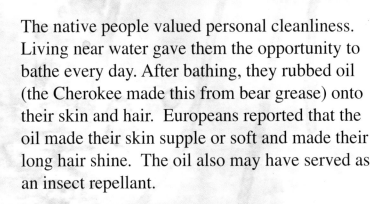

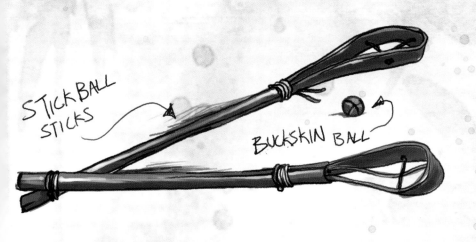

STICKBALL STICKS

BUCKSKIN BALL

The native people valued personal cleanliness. Living near water gave them the opportunity to bathe every day. After bathing, they rubbed oil (the Cherokee made this from bear grease) onto their skin and hair. Europeans reported that the oil made their skin supple or soft and made their long hair shine. The oil also may have served as an insect repellant.

Catawba men bathing and oiling their bodies

REGIONAL DIFFERENCES AMONG SOUTH CAROLINA TRIBES

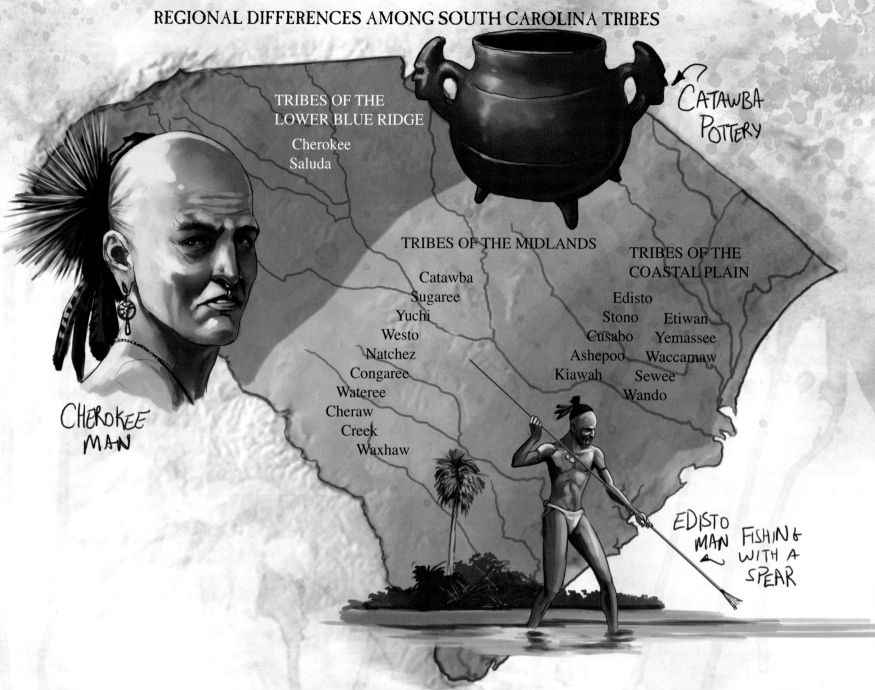

CATAWBA POTTERY

TRIBES OF THE
LOWER BLUE RIDGE

Cherokee
Saluda

TRIBES OF THE MIDLANDS

Catawba
Sugaree
Yuchi
Westo
Natchez
Congaree
Wateree
Cheraw
Creek
Waxhaw

TRIBES OF THE
COASTAL PLAIN

Edisto
Stono   Etiwan
Cusabo   Yemassee
Ashepoo   Waccamaw
Kiawah   Sewee
            Wando

CHEROKEE MAN

EDISTO MAN FISHING WITH A SPEAR

Native people lived in South Carolina's three distinct regions: The Coastal Plain, The Midlands (or Sandhills) and The Lower Blue Ridge Mountains. There were several sub-regions within each of the greater regions as well.

The 30 or so native tribes living in South Carolina before European contact settled in each of these three regions and adapted to the different living conditions they faced. The regions required different hunting methods, dress, customs and dwelling styles. Each tribe also had a unique dialect or way of talking based on ancestral origin. They talked like their ancestors who had come to South Carolina from different parts of present-day America and who fell into three distinct language families: Iroquoian, Muskogean and Siouan.

PEOPLE OF THE COASTAL REGION

The coastal tribes of native people lived in the Coastal Plain, a region that spans from the Atlantic coast to about 50 miles inland. This region is almost flat with dark fertile soils and slow-moving streams of black water colored by chemicals called tannins from decaying leaves. Trees in the region were primarily pine, live oak, tupelo and cypress.

The native people that lived between present-day Savannah and Charleston were collectively called Cusabos, and are thought to be of the Muskogean language family. These people likely arrived in South Carolina from present-day Georgia, Alabama and Florida. Examples of these tribes were the Kiawah, Edisto, Escamacu, Etiwan, Wimbee, Coosa, Stono, Ashepoo, Combahee and Yemassee.

Other tribes north of present-day Charleston are thought by scholars to have ancestors from the American Great Plains, and their language family was Siouan. Examples of tribes living in this subregion of the Coastal Plain were the Sewee, Santee, Pee Dee, Waccamaw, Winyah, Wando and Sampit.

The coastal tribes had dwellings called wigwams which looked a little like beehives and were domed structures made of wooden poles tied together and usually covered with palmetto fronds (leaves of palmetto trees). Most coastal tribes lived near the beach in the summer, but moved about 20 to 30 miles inland during the fall and winter months to escape mosquitoes and hurricanes.

Coastal village with dwellings and dugout canoes

Cusabo men hunting fish with a bow and arrow from a dugout canoe

Their summer life on the coast consisted of fishing and gathering food from the sea, such as oysters, clams, crabs and shrimp.

Cusabo woman picking berries wearing a garment made of Spanish moss

In the fall and winter the coastal tribes hunted animals such as deer and turkey and gathered nuts, including acorns.

PEOPLE OF THE MIDLANDS REGION

Tribes that lived farther inland in the Midlands Region include Catawba, Cheraw, Congaree, Wateree, Waxhaw and Sugaree. These tribes were known for their farming abilities and great endurance in battle. The Midlands Region has rolling hills of mostly sandy soils with oak, pine, poplar, sycamore and hickory trees.

Catawba village in the Midlands Region

Most tribes built their villages near streams and cultivated their crops of corn, squash and beans along the fertile bottomland. Game for food consisted of deer, rabbit, squirrel and other small animals. Dwellings usually were domed or rectangular structures much like those of the coastal tribes, except the roof was made of bark with a hole near the center for smoke to escape from the fire inside.

Catwba dwelling and couple

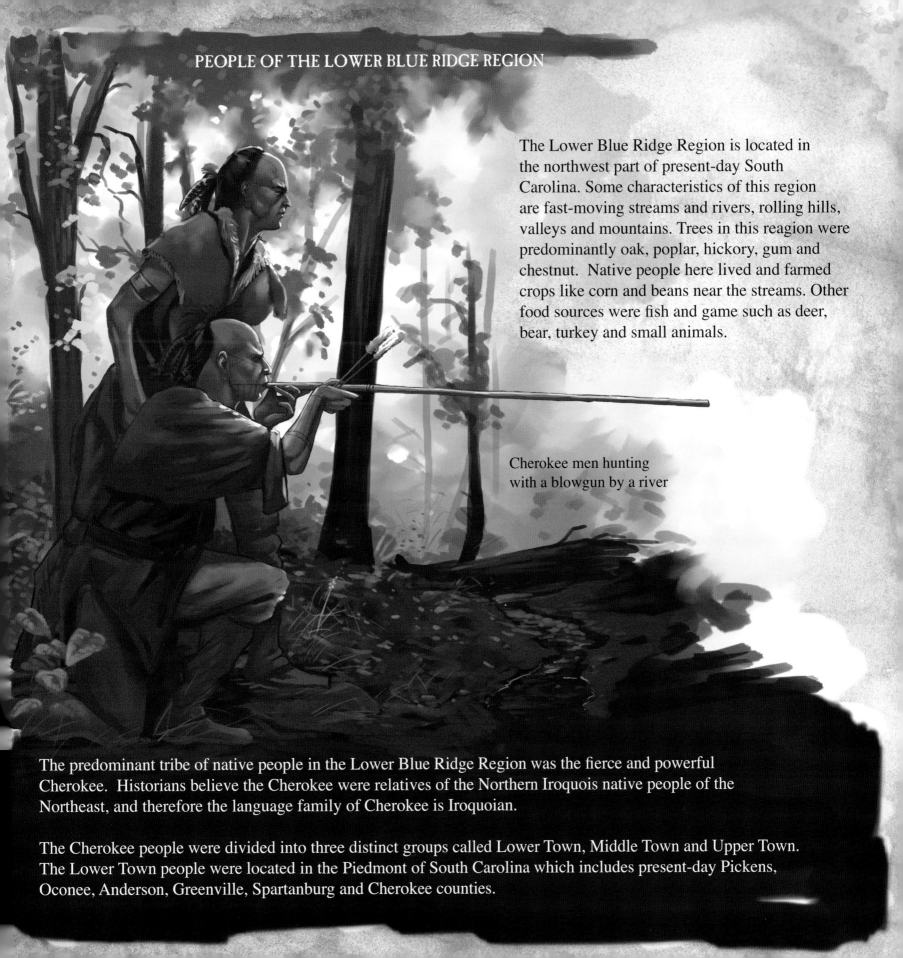

The Lower Blue Ridge Region is located in the northwest part of present-day South Carolina. Some characteristics of this region are fast-moving streams and rivers, rolling hills, valleys and mountains. Trees in this reagion were predominantly oak, poplar, hickory, gum and chestnut. Native people here lived and farmed crops like corn and beans near the streams. Other food sources were fish and game such as deer, bear, turkey and small animals.

Cherokee men hunting with a blowgun by a river

The predominant tribe of native people in the Lower Blue Ridge Region was the fierce and powerful Cherokee. Historians believe the Cherokee were relatives of the Northern Iroquois native people of the Northeast, and therefore the language family of Cherokee is Iroquoian.

The Cherokee people were divided into three distinct groups called Lower Town, Middle Town and Upper Town. The Lower Town people were located in the Piedmont of South Carolina which includes present-day Pickens, Oconee, Anderson, Greenville, Spartanburg and Cherokee counties.

The Cherokee lived in cabins constructed with wooden poles. The walls consisted of woven wood strips, which formed a lattice. This was "daubed" (covered) inside and out with smooth clay. The roof was made of narrow boards or bark from trees such as chestnut. The Cherokee also built corncribs or other structures to store their crops and protect them from rain and pests, such as rats, mice and insects.

Cherokee men making a dugout canoe in front of a dwelling

SOCIAL STRUCTURE

Most tribes in the low country had Kings, or Caciques. Some of the coastal tribes had women chiefs, called Queens. Other tribes had chiefs. Their role in society was primarily ceremonial, and they mainly governed by public opinion. Much like today's small towns, almost all personal interactions among individuals were public knowledge.

Cherokee Chief

Cherokee family

Whenever fights broke out and there were injuries or deaths, people often sought revenge. The chief and village elders (similar to current-day town council) tried hard to keep peace and prevent a quarrel from spreading. Native people who committed offenses suffered disapproval or were shunned by the village.

In most tribes the women did most of the field work, including planting, cultivating and harvesting crops for food. The men hunted or prepared for playing games, conducting ceremonies or going into battle. Families consisted of a father and mother and usually only one or two children.

COUNCIL OR TOWN HOUSE

Every tribe had a large central gathering place in the center of the village called the Council or Town House. It is comparable to today's City Hall or County Court House. Inside the Council House it was dark except for light from a fire, surrounded by rows of seats raised like an amphitheater.

In a Cherokee Council House, men sat around smoking pipes and discussing village business while women moved to and from the fields outside with baskets of vegetables or carrying water from the stream.

Council house

Men gathered inside a Council House smoking and talking

RELIGIOUS TRADITION

Native people believed in communication with the spirits of the animal and plant world. For example, when a man killed a wild animal or caught a fish, he asked its spirit to pardon him. He didn't want the spirits to deny him good hunting or fishing in the future. The people believed that every living thing has a spirit and all things are important for balance and harmony in the natural world.

Cherokee hunters with a killed black bear

Cherokee shaman praying over a dead man

The sun, the moon, fire and water formed an important basis of the religious beliefs of native people. The Cherokee, for example, prayed to the sun to bring abundant crops and good health. They believed that fire had been appointed by the sun and moon to take care of the people. Most native people believed in an afterlife where those who behaved well went to a light and pleasant place.

The medicine man or shaman was the religious leader of the village, and was like a preacher or minister since he communicated the relationships between the physical and spiritual aspects of native life and culture. Medicine men knew about plants that were used to cure sickness. Sometimes the religious leader and the medicine man were two different people. The Cherokee used a plant called snakeroot to cure snakebites and "nervousness," and a dark tea made from sassafras roots to cure digestive problems and headaches.

FOOD FOR NATIVE PEOPLE

Food for the coastal tribes consisted of seafood like oysters, clams, shrimp, crabs and fish during the spring and summer, along with corn, vegetables and melons. The people were expert fishermen, and used nets, traps or bows to spear fish such as sturgeon, trout, flounder and red drum in the marsh. In the fall these people moved inland and changed their diets to include deer, small animals and wild turkey, as well as dried meat and acorns.

OYSTERS

REDFISH

STURGEON

CUSABO MAN WITH HIS CATCH

Hunter taking aim

FISH TRAP

HICKORY NUTS

CHESTNUTS

BLOWGUN + DARTS

In the Midlands, native people grew corn, beans, squash and melons. For meat, they hunted animals using spears, bows and arrows or traps. Traps were also used to catch fish in the streams. The native people of the foothills of the Blue Ridge Mountains farmed corn and other vegetables on the fertile bottomland soils along the rivers and creeks. The Cherokee hunted deer, wild turkey, bear and small game.

They hunted large animals with spears or bows and arrows. They hollowed out river cane to make blowguns and used darts made from the stems of certain plants to hunt small animals such as birds, squirrel and rabbit. In the winter months the people ate stored food and gathered acorns, hickory nuts and walnuts.

In order to provide food for deer and turkey, the people used controlled burning to thin out the weeds and brush, allowing sunlight to reach wild grasses which provided ample food for game animals.

DRIED DEER MEAT

Native men burning underbrush

The people either boiled or roasted fish and shellfish (oysters, shrimp and clams). They usually cooked or barbequed deer on a wooden frame over a slow fire. Dried deer meat and fish were important food sources for native people in the winter months, and for people traveling long distances.

Roasting meat over an open fire

HUNTING TOOLS

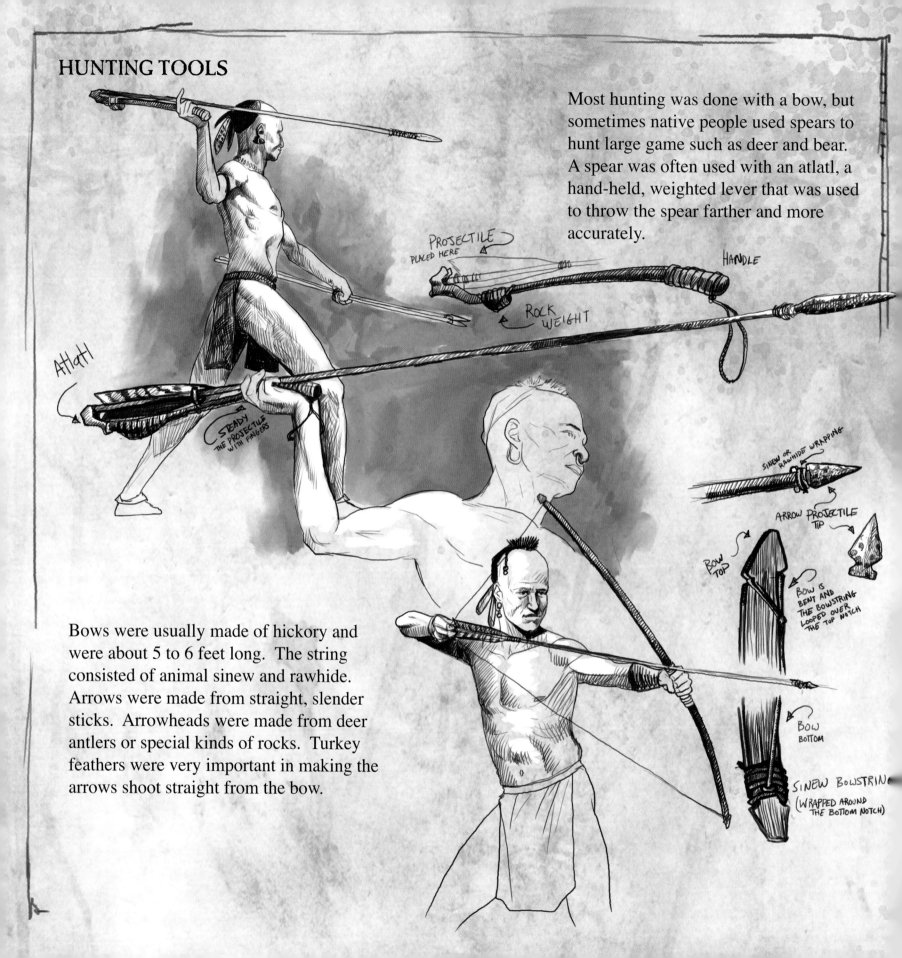

Most hunting was done with a bow, but sometimes native people used spears to hunt large game such as deer and bear. A spear was often used with an atlatl, a hand-held, weighted lever that was used to throw the spear farther and more accurately.

PROJECTILE PLACED HERE

HANDLE

ROCK WEIGHT

AtlatI

STEADY THE PROJECTILE WITH FINGERS

SINEW OR RAWHIDE WRAPPING

ARROW PROJECTILE TIP

BOW TOP

BOW IS BENT AND THE BOWSTRING LOOPED OVER THE TOP NOTCH

Bows were usually made of hickory and were about 5 to 6 feet long. The string consisted of animal sinew and rawhide. Arrows were made from straight, slender sticks. Arrowheads were made from deer antlers or special kinds of rocks. Turkey feathers were very important in making the arrows shoot straight from the bow.

BOW BOTTOM

SINEW BOWSTRING (WRAPPED AROUND THE BOTTOM NOTCH)

USING CROPS FOR FOOD

The most important crop cultivated by native people was corn, also known as maize. Corn came to the Southeast from Central America where it was grown by the Aztec and Mayan Indians several thousand years ago.

Native people of current South Carolina used corn in several ways. They used the kernels for food, and the husks for masks, baskets, sleeping mats and even dolls. The cobs were used for fuel and to make rattles.

Corn was harvested in the milky stage for roasting, and dried kernels were made into corn meal and hominy. Hominy, like grits, was made by soaking the dried kernels in a wood ash-water mixture until they split. Dried hominy could be stored or carried by the men when going hunting or into battle. Corn meal, made by pounding dried corn kernels with a hard piece of wood or stone, could be made into cornbread, corn syrup or corn pudding. Beans or peas were often mixed with corn to make succotash. Other important crops were pumpkin, squash, melons and gourds. Berries, chestnuts, acorns, hickory nuts and walnuts were gathered from the forests and fields around the villages and consumed mostly in winter when other food was scarce.

Acorns were pressed into paste and used to thicken soups or broth. Hickory nuts were beaten and boiled, and the oil that floated to the top was used for cooking and as a skin moisturizer. Wild fruit, like persimmon, was pressed into cakes and dried for winter eating.

TRANSPORTATION

Since most native people lived near water, the canoe was the most important means of transportation. Some canoes were short and made for only 2 or 3 people, but others were long (up to 30 feet), and could carry up to 10 people. Canoes were made of hollowed out logs of cypress (coastal tribes) or poplar (Cherokee). Native people used a sharp tool, such as an oyster shell or rock, to chip away the wood to make a sitting space, then lit a fire to burn away more wood. They repeated this until the canoe's sitting area was acceptable.

For traveling across land to hunt, gather food, do battle or just to visit other villages, native people used well-traveled trails where possible. They had great endurance and could travel distances of 10 to 20 miles in a day at a slow, steady run. In fact, modern-day fitness experts patterned "jogging" after this type of running.

GAMES AND RECREATION

Two games were very important in the social lives of the native people. Both were played in the village courtyard close to the Council House.

Chunkey was played with a round, smooth and polished flat stone resembling a hockey puck. The object of the game was for two players to roll the chunkey stone down a smooth and packed dirt surface while they threw long poles to see who could come closest to the stone. Chiefs or elite warriors usually won.

CHUNKEY PLAYER FIGURINE

The other game was stickball, played much like today's lacrosse, but with two short sticks about 2 to 3 feet long, one in each hand. At the end of each stick was a small cup made of strips of deerskin leather. Stickball was played with two teams, both trying to get the small ball, made of a stone covered in deerskin, across the goal line of the other team. A goal was scored if the ball hit a pole or was shot between two poles. Games were very physical and often resulted in injuries. Villages had stickball teams and games between teams were watched by lots of people. Each team had a leader or "captain" – usually a well-known warrior. Today, the Cherokee still play stickball at annual tribal fairs.

STICKBALL STICK
MADE OF WOOD + SINEW

BUCKSKIN
BALL

STICKBALL
PLAYER

THE GREEN CORN CEREMONY

The Green Corn Ceremony or The Busk was usually held for four to eight days in August after the green corn ears were harvested. It was the celebration of the good crop and a time of renewal. Native people put out the fires in their dwellings and in the council house. They fasted for three days, then they sang, danced, feasted and re-lit the ceremonial fires in the village square and in their homes. For some tribes, such as the Cherokee, the Green Corn Ceremony was a time for all to forgive grudges, debts and minor crimes.

CONFLICT AND WARFARE

Native people were generally not warlike, except in cases of revenge. In such situations, a war party would be sent to avenge the wrongdoing. Before going into battle, the warriors usually would coat themselves with bear grease and a reddish body paint made from a plant root.

CATAWBA WARRIOR

Warriors would decorate their heads with feathers, and paint their faces in various patterns, such as a circle of black around one eye and a circle of red around the other. Before European contact, weapons were primarily the bow and arrow, but tomahawks were used for close hand-to-hand combat.

Cherokee warrior stalking his enemies—

CARVED WAR CLUB

DEER ANTLER POINT

ROCK TOMAHAWK

SINEW + PITCH TIE STONE TO STICK

SMOOTH RIVER STONE

EUROPEAN CONTACT WITH NATIVE AMERICANS

Hernando de Soto and Spanish explorers meeting the Lady of Cofitachequi, a woman chief, by the Wateree River near present-day Camden

The first Europeans to contact Native Americans in present-day South Carolina were from Spain and France. They came to the New World seeking riches like gold, silver and precious stones. They were also interested in capturing people to use as slaves to work on plantations in the West Indies.

Sadly, the European explorers, such as Hernando de Soto, brought things that would threaten the very existence of the Native Americans. Germs brought by the Europeans caused great sickness and death among the natives. Europeans had developed immunity or resistance to diseases like smallpox, measles and diphtheria, but the native people of America had no immunity. They suffered and died in great numbers. The Europeans brought pigs that caused disease and crop losses from their rooting and digging. Europeans also brought guns, knives and rum, which would forever change the lives and social structure of the Native Americans.

Other Spanish and French explorers followed de Soto.

By 1670, when the English arrived in the Charleston area, disease and war with the Europeans had already reduced the numbers of native people. There were not many left to defend their tribal lands.

GLOSSARY

Atlatl – a short (2-3 ft.) shaft with a cup or spur at the end that native people attached to a spear to make it go farther and faster.

Blowgun – a 4-6 ft. long piece of hollowed out river cane that native people used to blow darts at small game animals.

Bottomland – flat land with rich fertile soil next to streams where native people cultivated their crops.

The Busk or Green Corn Ceremony – celebration of native people in late summer when corn is ready for harvest.

Cacique – the chief of some low country South Carolina tribes.

Chunkey – a game in which spears were thrown at a smooth round disc-shaped stone rolled along a smooth surface – winner was closest to where the stone stopped.

Council House – where native people conducted business of the village or tribe.

Dialect – a way of speaking, characteristic of a village or tribe.

Europeans – people from countries in Europe, such as Spain, France and England, who came to North America seeking a route to India.

Hernando de Soto – A Spanish explorer who landed in present-day Florida in 1539 and moved with his force throughout the Southeast and finally across the Mississippi River.

Hominy – corn kernels that were soaked in a wood ash/water mixture, then dried and crushed. Native people added water to make a soup-like food like our grits.

Ice Age – a period several thousand years ago when ice sheets covered large portions of the earth, including the area between today's Siberia (Russia) and Alaska, over which early people traveled to the North American continent.

Immunity – resistance to disease or infection.

Iroquois – the name of the language family of the Cherokee, who were descendents of the Iroquois native people of the northeastern area of current US.

Jogging – a slow run used by native people to travel sometimes 10 to 20 miles a day on hunts or to do battle.

Language family – a group of languages that native people have in common. There were about seven different language families in North America. In South Carolina, there were three main language families: Iroquoian, Siouan and Muskogean.

GLOSSARY

Lye – a substance made by native people from wood ashes to use in soaking dried corn kernels to make hominy.

Maize – another word for corn, the main crop of the native people of South Carolina.

Mississippian Period – a time period roughly 500 to 1,000 years ago in current South Carolina, during which native people built villages on hills or bluffs along rivers – also characterized by mound building.

Moccasins – shoes made from deerskins.

Muskogean – language family of several tribes of native people who lived between current Savannah and Charleston. Scholars believe they are descendents of people who came from the southwest through the current southern states of Louisiana, Mississippi, Alabama and Georgia. Examples are the Kiawah, Edisto, Wando, Combahee and Yemassee tribes.

Shaman – religious leader of the village or tribe, sometimes also known for his knowledge of plants used to treat various illnesses or conditions.

Sinew - A piece of tough fibrous tissue uniting muscle to bone or bone to bone; a tendon or ligament.

Siouan – language family of certain South Carolina native tribes (e.g., Catawba and Waccamaw) whose ancestors were from the Great Plains of the current US.

Slavery – system under which people were captured, bought or sold, and forced to work against their will. Some native people were sold into slavery.

Snake root – root used by native people to make a healing tea with which they treated snakebites and various digestive problems.

Spanish moss – a plant used by early people for clothing that gets nutrients and water from the air and grows on the limbs of live oaks and cypress trees in the Coastal Plain of South Carolina.

Stickball – a game in which players used a stick – one in each hand – to pass a ball with the object of hitting a goal post or passing it between two goal posts – much like today's lacrosse.

Tannins – chemicals from rotting plant materials, such as leaves, which cause water in low country rivers of South Carolina (e.g., the Edisto) to appear black.

Tattooing – a form of body decoration made by inserting a dye or ink into the outer layer of skin with a sharp instrument or tool – some native people used tattooing to identify their tribes or to celebrate victory in battle.

Woodland Period – a time roughly 2,000 to 3,000 years ago for the area of current South Carolina, during which native people began firing clay pottery and cultivating crops.

BIBLIOGRAPHY

Bierer, Bert W. *South Carolina Indian Lore*. Published by Bert W. Bierer. Columbia, SC. 1972.

Edgar, Walter. *South Carolina: A History*. University of South Carolina Press. Columbia, SC. 1998.

Hamel, Paul B. and Mary U. Chiltoskey. *Cherokee Plants – Their Uses, a 400 Year History.* Booklet published by authors in 1975.

Hudson, Charles M. *Southeastern Indians.* University of Tennessee Press. Knoxville, Tennessee. 1978.

Lawson, John. *A New Voyage to Carolina.* Publisher Unknown. London, England. 1709.

Milling, Chapman J. With Forward by A. S. Salley. *Red Carolinians.* University of South Carolina Press. Columbia, SC. 1969.

Waddell, Gene. *Indians of the South Carolina Lowcountry, 1562-1751.* Southern Studies Program, University of South Carolina. Columbia, SC. 1980.

Wallace, David Duncan. *South Carolina: A Short History, 1520-1948.* University of South Carolina Press. Columbia, SC. 1961

THE AUTHORS

Kate Salley Palmer

Kate is a former nationally syndicated political cartoonist who started writing and illustrating children's picture books in 1991. Her first two books were published by Simon and Schuster – *A Gracious Plenty* and *How Many Feet in the Bed* (Author, Diane Johnston Hamm). She has since illustrated books for Boyds Mills Press, Albert Whitman and Kaeden. In 1998, Kate and her husband, Jim, started Warbranch Press, Inc., and their first book was a soft cover edition of *A Gracious Plenty*, which is a family story about Kate's great-aunt May Zeigler. This book was followed by *The Pink House* and *The Little Chairs* – also about Kate's family. In 2005, Warbranch Press, started its current series of picture books about South Carolina history by publishing *Palmetto – Symbol of Courage*, the story of how the state's beautiful state flag came to be. Later that same year, Kate wrote the story of the state's most famous Revolutionary War hero, Francis Marion. Her son, James, did the vivid digital illustrations for *Francis Marion and the Legend of the Swamp Fox*. During one of her many school author visits, Kate was asked the following question by a 3rd grader: "Were there any black heroes from the Revolution?" Kate said there probably were, and that she would do research and possibly write a book about the subject. In 2009, she wrote and illustrated *Almost Invisible – Black Patriots of the American Revolution*. She has also written her political cartoon memoir, *Growing Up Cartoonist in the Baby Boom South*, published in 2006 by the Clemson University Digital Press. Kate speaks about her books at schools, conferences and other groups. She and Jim live in Clemson, South Carolina.

Jim Palmer

Jim is Emeritus Professor of Agronomy at Clemson University. His career at Clemson consisted of Extension, research and teaching in the area of sustainable cropping systems. After retirement, Jim devoted his energies to the marketing and business activities of Warbranch Press, Inc. He says that he logistical facets of running a publishing company can be challenging, but also very exciting. Warbranch Press has published six books, and has sold over 50,000 copies of these and Kate's books by other publishers. *First South Carolinians* is Jim's first as co-author with Kate.

THE ILLUSTRATOR

James H. Palmer Jr.

James, Jim and Kate's son, grew up in Clemson. James graduated with a Bachelor's degree in English from Clemson University in 1993. Since 1998, James has been working as an illustrator and graphic artist in Atlanta, Georgia. *First South Carolinians* is the second book he's illustrated for Warbranch Press. His first, *Francis Marion and the Legend of the Swamp Fox,* is in its 3rd printing, and is the press's top-selling book. James is also the illustrator for two SC ETV film documentaries – *Chasing the Swamp Fox* (2005) and *Forgotten Founder* (2010) . James's full-time job is working as an artist with The Graphic Cow in Liberty, SC. He continues to freelance--creating art and other graphics for a variety of clients. James's wife, Mandy is co-founder of The Nest Nursery School in Atlanta. James and Mandy's son Leo is currently in first grade at Parkside Elementary and seems to be sharing his dad's love of art and strorytelling.